I0399816

This Planner Belongs To:

Wish. Plan. Party

BOOKFLY PUBLISHING

Calendar

SUN	MON	TUE	WED	THU	FRI	SAT

NOTES

The Plan

Celebrating: _____
Party Theme: _____
Adults Invited: _____ Children Invited: _____

PARTY DETAILS

Location: _____

Address: _____
_____

Date: _____ Time: _____

Phone: _____

Email/Website: _____

INVITATIONS

Invitations Needed: # _____

Mail by: _____

○ Ordered: _____ ○ Making: _____

_____
_____

MENU

_____
_____
_____
_____

DECORATIONS

○ _____
○ _____
○ _____
○ _____

FAVORS

○ _____
○ _____
○ _____
○ _____

ENTERTAINMENT/GAMES/ACTIVITIES

○ _____
○ _____
○ _____
○ _____

The Checklist

Celebrating: _____ Date: _____ Budget: _____
Party Theme: _____ Colors: _____
Location: _____ Adults Invited: _____ Children Invited: _____

6 WEEKS

4 WEEKS

3 WEEKS

2 WEEKS

NOTES

The Budget

VENUE & ENTERTAINMENT	BUDGET	ACTUAL

FOOD & DRINKS		

DECORATIONS & STATIONARY		

ACTIVITIES & GAMES		
	BUDGET TOTAL	ACTUAL TOTAL
	$	$

The Decorations

THEME ELEMENTS

SHOPPING LIST

IDEAS

TABLE DECORATIONS

DECORATIONS TO MAKE

The Menu

APPETIZERS & SNACKS

MAIN COURSE

SIDE DISHES

CAKE & DESSERTS

SHOPPING LIST

DRINKS

Party Vendors

VENDOR CONTACT LIST

Name: Address:
www.   Phone: Fax:
Contact Person: Phone: Email:
Service Provided: Cost: $ ⭕ Paid
Notes:

Name: Address:
www.   Phone: Fax:
Contact Person: Phone: Email:
Service Provided: Cost: $ ⭕ Paid
Notes:

Name: Address:
www.   Phone: Fax:
Contact Person: Phone: Email:
Service Provided: Cost: $ ⭕ Paid
Notes:

Name: Address:
www.   Phone: Fax:
Contact Person: Phone: Email:
Service Provided: Cost: $ ⭕ Paid
Notes:

Invitation List

Name: Address: Attending
Parent: Phone: Allergies: ○

Name: Address: Attending
Parent: Phone: Allergies: ○

Name: Address: Attending
Parent: Phone: Allergies: ○

Name: Address: Attending
Parent: Phone: Allergies: ○

Name: Address: Attending
Parent: Phone: Allergies: ○

Name: Address: Attending
Parent: Phone: Allergies: ○

Name: Address: Attending
Parent: Phone: Allergies: ○

Name: Address: Attending
Parent: Phone: Allergies: ○

Name: Address: Attending
Parent: Phone: Allergies: ○

Invitation List

Name:	Address:		Attending
Parent:	Phone:	Allergies:	○

Name:	Address:		Attending
Parent:	Phone:	Allergies:	○

Name:	Address:		Attending
Parent:	Phone:	Allergies:	○

Name:	Address:		Attending
Parent:	Phone:	Allergies:	○

Name:	Address:		Attending
Parent:	Phone:	Allergies:	○

Name:	Address:		Attending
Parent:	Phone:	Allergies:	○

Name:	Address:		Attending
Parent:	Phone:	Allergies:	○

Name:	Address:		Attending
Parent:	Phone:	Allergies:	○

Name:	Address:		Attending
Parent:	Phone:	Allergies:	○

Games & Favors

ENTERTAINMENT

Name:

Description:

Start Time: EndTime:

Notes:

GAMES & ACTIVITIES

Activity:

Details:

Prize:

Activity:

Details:

Prize:

PARTY FAVORS

Favors Needed: #   Box/Bag:

Label/Tag:

FILLER ITEMS

SHOPPING LIST

-
-
-
-
-
-
-
-
-
-
-

The Music Playlist

SONG TITLE	ARTIST

INTERMISSION NUMBER

Master Shopping List

| FOOD & DRINK | DECORATIONS & STATIONARY | FAVORS & PRIZES |

| TABLEWARE & PAPER GOODS | ACTIVITIES & GAMES | MISCELLANEOUS ITEMS |

My Wish List

Name:
Birthday: Age:

I'M REALLY HOPING FOR:

THINGS I REALLY LOVE

THINGS I REALLY NEED

FAVORITES

Color:
Books:
Movie:
Other:

Party Day

SCHEDULE

ERRANDS

FOOD PREP

SET UP

NOTES

The Gifts

GIFT	FROM	THANK YOU

Birthday Interview

Today is: _____ and I am _____ years old!

My favorite color is: _____

My favorite animal is: _____

My favorite TV show is: _____

My favorite food is: _____

My favorite movie is: _____

I like to play: _____

My favorite place to go is: _____

I am scared of: _____

My best friend is: _____

Something I like to do is: _____

Something I like to think about is: _____

When I grow up I want to be: _____

_____

Attach photo here

I like to draw...

Party Memories

ATTACH PHOTO HERE

About this photo _____

_____
_____
_____
_____
_____

Countdown Blocks

Copyright© 2022 by Bookfly Publishing

No part of this publication may be reproduced, stored in a retrieval system, or transmitted in any form or by any means, electronic, mechanical, photocopying, recording, or otherwise, without the written permission of the publisher.

Limited Liability/Disclaimer of Warranty. The publisher and the author make no representation or warranties with the respect to the accuracy or completeness of the contents of this work and specifically disclaim all warranties including without limitation warranties for a particular purpose. No warranty may be created or extended by sales or promotional materials. The advice or strategies contained herein may not be suitable for every situation. This work is sold with the understanding that the publisher is not engaged in rendering medical, legal, or other professional advice or services. Neither the publisher nor the author or creator shall be liable for damages arising.

For general information on our other products and services please visit www.bookflypublishing.com or contact our Customer Care Department at info@bookflypublishing.com.

Bookfly Publishing publishes its books and materials in a variety of electronic and print formats. Some content that appears in print may not be available in electronic books and vice versa.

ISBN 978-1-7369393-7-6
All rights reserved. Published by Bookfly Publishing
Harvey, Louisiana
www.bookflypublishing.com

Printed in the USA

www.ingramcontent.com/pod-product-compliance
Lightning Source LLC
Chambersburg PA
CBHW050747110526
44590CB00003B/105